AF245536

God's Mustard Seed
Volume 1

Written by Joan Kile

Illustrated by Teresa Ragland from picture
ideas drawn by The Mustard Seed Kids

Musty the Mustard Seed Books (MMSB)

Cover design by Teresa Ragland
Illustrations by Teresa Ragland

GOD'S MUSTARD SEED
© 1993 by Joan Kile
Published by Musty the Mustard Seed Books (MMSB)
104 Stable Court
Franklin, TN 37064

Printed in the United States of America

First Edition, 1993

Printed by Arcata Graphics/Kingsport
P.O. Box 711 (Press St.)
Kingsport, TN 37662

ISBN 0-9636314-0-3

God's Mustard Seed is
dedicated to all the children
whose prayers helped make
a dream become a reality.

Musty the Mustard Seed,
filled with God's love, likes
to walk through the pages
of the Bible. Let's walk
with him!

Jesus said that the Kingdom
of God is like a grain of
mustard seed, which when sown
upon the ground is the smallest
of all seeds upon the earth;

Yet after it is sown it
grows up and becomes the
greatest of all garden herbs,
and puts out large branches,

**So that the birds of the air
are able to make nests and
dwell in its shade.** *(Mark 4:31–32, AMP)*

**Jesus said that the Kingdom of
Heaven is like a tiny mustard seed
planted in a field. It is the smallest
of all seeds, but becomes the largest
of plants, and grows into a tree where
birds can come and find shelter.**

(Matthew 13:31–32, TLB)

A mustard seed of Jesus' love
can be sown in your heart.

It can grow and grow and grow!

Other people will seek the love
of Jesus that they see in your
heart—your tree of Christianity.

The Bible tells us about Jesus' love.

Do you love to read the Bible?
Wouldn't it be wonderful if we
hungered to read our Bibles as
much or more than we hunger
for food?

The Bible tells us that
God loves us so much
that He sent His only
Son to earth. When
Jesus was on earth,
He loved to bless the
little children.

Once when some mothers were bringing their children to Jesus to bless them, the disciples shooed them away, telling them not to bother him.

But when Jesus saw what was happening he was very much displeased with his disciples and said to them, "Let the children come to me, for the Kingdom of God belongs to such as they. Don't send them away!

I tell you as seriously as I know how that anyone who refuses to come to God as a little child will never be allowed into his Kingdom.” *(Mark 10:13–15, TLB)*

Jesus wants us to come to Him for a blessing. We shouldn't wait to call upon Him when we are sick or in trouble. He wants to bless us now!

He will not let anyone
turn us away. We can
come to Jesus just the
way we are and He will
love us. What a joyous
message!

Let us come to God now and
ask Jesus into our hearts.

Father—

Let us come unto Jesus as
little children wanting His blessing.
Let nothing stop us from receiving
Jesus into our hearts.

Thank you for our Mustard Seed.
May it grow in your light and
in your way, dear Lord.

Amen

Musty the Mustard Seed
says, "God Bless You!"

**If ye have *faith* as a
grain of mustard seed . . .
nothing shall be impossible
unto you.** (*Matthew 17:20, KJV*)

Dear Boys and Girls,

Musty and I pray that reading *God's Mustard Seed* brought you into a closer relationship with Jesus. Have you asked the Lord Jesus to forgive your sins? Have you told Him that you believe He died on the cross for your sins? Have you asked Jesus to come into your heart and live with you?

Pray each day in the name of Jesus. Read your Bible. Tell other people about Jesus.

God bless you and your family!

Love,
Miss Joan

P.S. Musty wants you to memorize the verses from the Bible on the next pages and say a verse each day.

I am come that they might have life, and that they might have it more abundantly.
(John 10:10, KJV)

The Kingdom of God is within you.
(Luke 17:21, KJV)

28

The things which
are impossible with
men are possible
with God.
(Luke 18:27, KJV)

What things soever
ye desire, when ye
pray, believe that ye
receive them, and ye
shall have them.
(Mark 11:24, KJV)

If thou canst believe, all things are possible to him that believeth.
(Mark 9:23, KJV)
I can do all things through Christ which strengtheneth me.
(Philippians 4:13, KJV)

Joan Kile wanted to be a teacher all her life. At five years of age, she "lined up her dolls and took attendance." Her mother says that she was born to be a teacher, always playing school while growing up on a farm in Ohio. Joan's dream was realized when she taught for over 20 years in both public and private schools. She has a Master of Education Degree in Early Childhood Education from Middle Tennessee State University. Joan and her husband, Burke, live in Franklin, Tennessee.

Joan's idea for Musty the Mustard Seed Books was conceived during the three years that she wrote, narrated, directed, and produced The Mustard Seed Gospel Radio Program in Nashville, Tennessee. She did the voice of Musty the Mustard Seed. These books are written from the scripts of the radio programs. Many children who participated in the radio programs drew picture ideas for the illustrations of Musty the Mustard Seed Books.

Joan's son, Grant Cole, was one of the children that had a part in The Mustard Seed radio programs. Grant and his wife, Susan, live in Alexandria, Virginia. She has two grown step-sons, Steve and Chris Kile.

She has used Musty the Mustard Seed Books with great success in teaching Sunday School. Joan's vision is for Musty the Mustard Seed Books to be used in teaching the gospel message to children throughout the world!

Books To Follow *God's Mustard Seed*